THREE STRATEGIES OF HUANG SHIGONG

A MILITARY CLASSIC FROM ANCIENT CHINA

Cherry Stone Publishing, an imprint of
Sweet Cherry Publishing Limited
Unit 36, Vulcan House,
Vulcan Road,
Leicester, LE5 3EF
United Kingdom

First published by Cherry Stone Publishing in 2021
2021 edition

2 4 6 8 10 9 7 5 3 1

ISBN: 978-1-78226-966-3

© Sweet Cherry Publishing

Three Strategies of Huang Shigong

All rights reserved. No part of this publication may be reproduced or utilised in any form or by any means, electronic or mechanical, including photocopying, recording, or using any information storage and retrieval system, without prior permission in writing from the publisher.

This book is copyright under the Berne Convention.
No reproduction without permission.
All rights reserved.

Cover design and illustrations
by Sophie Jones

www.cherrystonepublishing.com

Printed and bound in India
I.TP002

THREE STRATEGIES OF HUANG SHIGONG

A TREATISE ON MILITARY STRATEGY

CHERRY STONE PUBLISHING

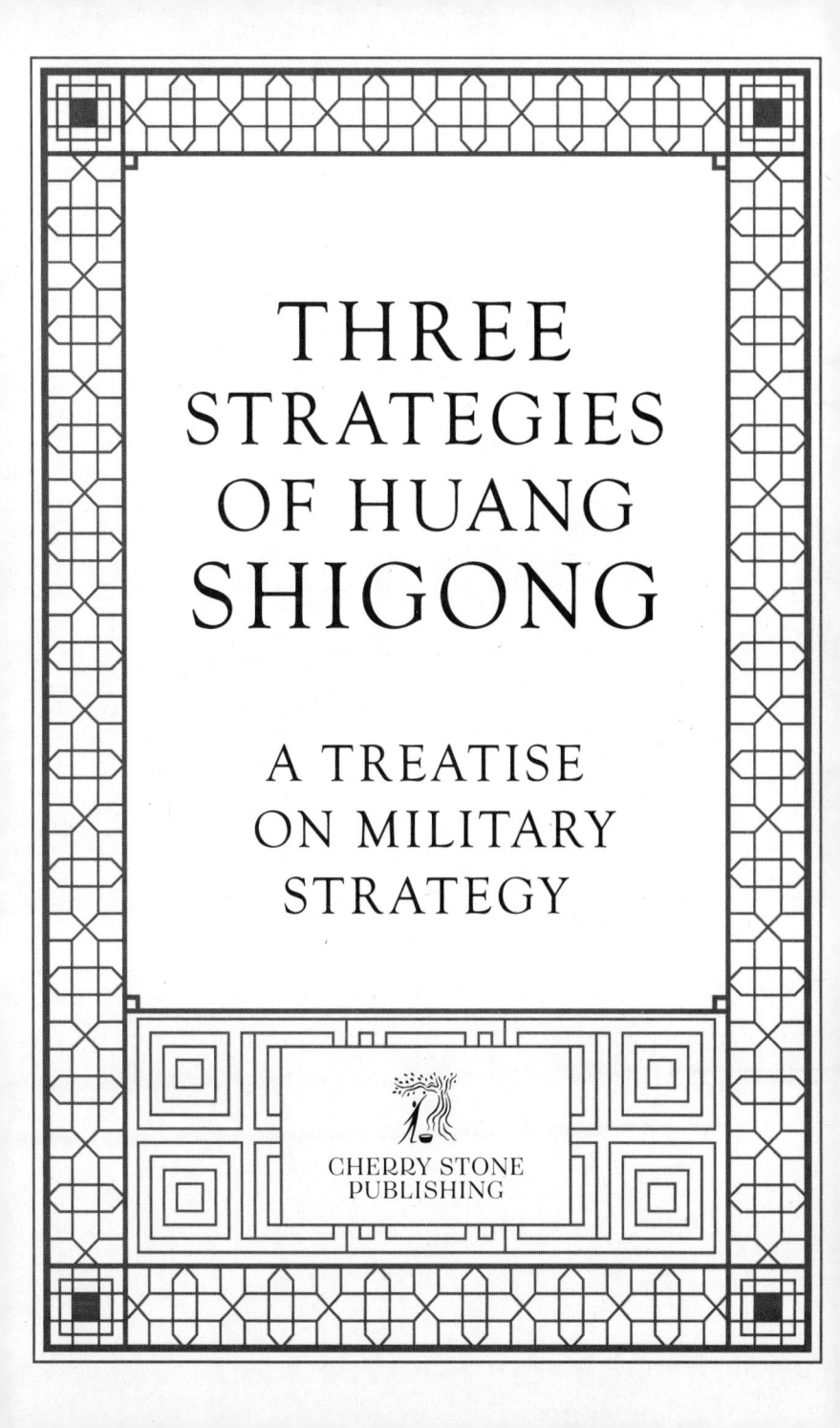

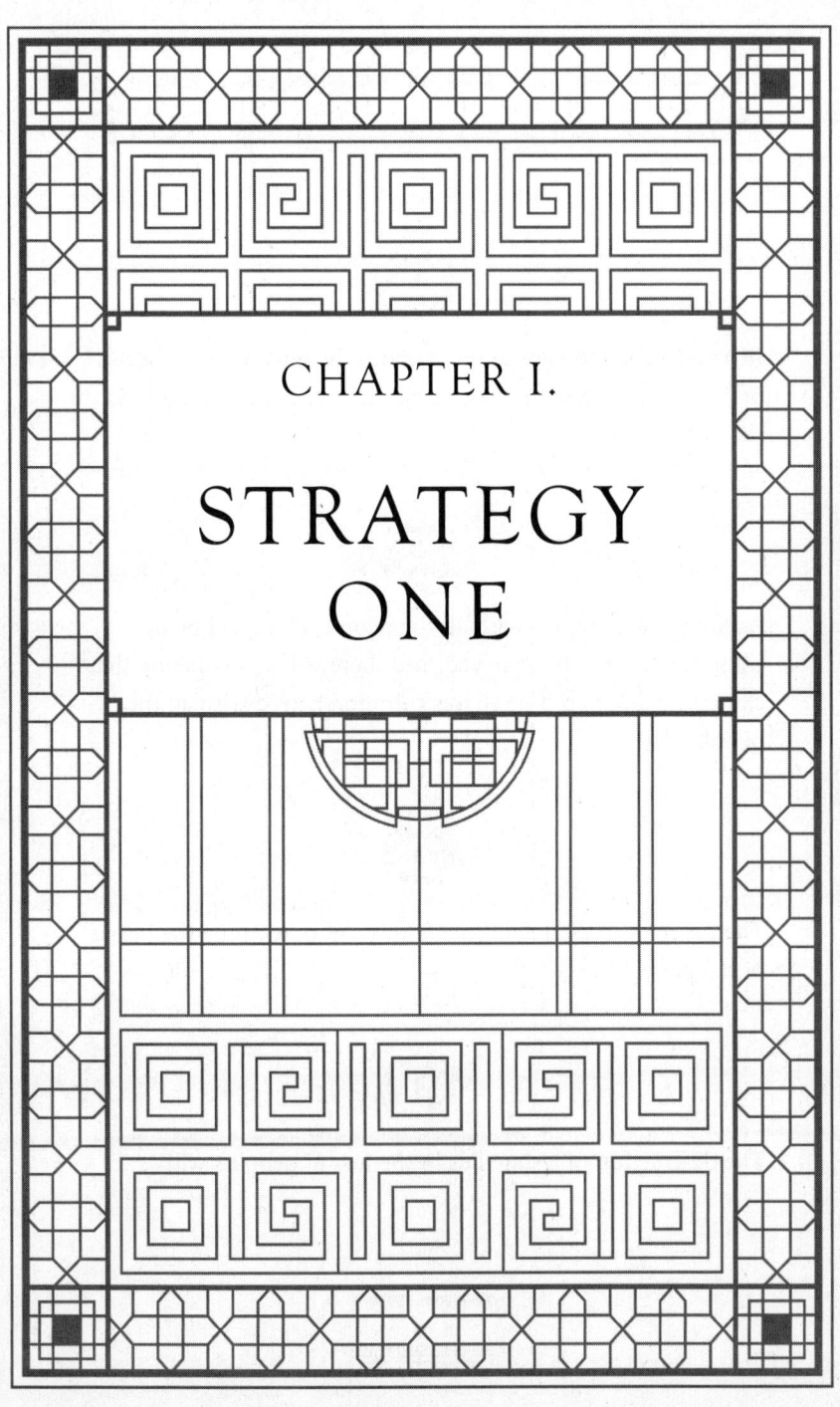

CHAPTER I.

STRATEGY ONE

THREE STRATEGIES OF HUANG SHIGONG

In a general's mind are these methods: he must win the hearts of heroes, reward meritorious officials, and connect his will with the public.

As long as his mind is with all the people, there will be no cause that cannot be achieved, and there will be no enemy that cannot be defeated if he shares common hatred with all the people.

The peace of the state and the family lies in winning the hearts of the people.

The destruction of a state lies in the loss of people's will.

STRATEGY ONE

People are willing to achieve their aspirations.

According to the ancient book of *Military Prophecy*: "the soft can control the strong, and the weak can control the strong as well." Softness is a virtue, but rigidity is a curse.

The weak are often sympathised with and supported by people while the strong are often resented and attacked by people.

Softness has the use of softness; rigidity has the use of rigidity; weakness has the use of weakness; and strength has the use of strength.

THREE STRATEGIES OF HUANG SHIGONG

We should skillfully combine these four aspects and apply them according to the circumstances.

Until the beginning and end of a thing is revealed, people can't anticipate it.

The law of heaven and earth changes with the development of the world; and the same is true of war.

Therefore, in military affairs, we should take appropriate counter-measures according to the changes of the enemy's situation.

STRATEGY ONE

We should not take action first until we grasp the situation.

In this way, we can plan to win, be invincible, assist the monarch, establish dignity, save the world and stabilise all sides.

The person who can make plans and give advice like this can be the teacher of the king.

There is no one who does not crave strength, but few can grasp the subtle truth: softness can overcome hardness and weakness can overcome strength.

THREE STRATEGIES OF HUANG SHIGONG

To be more specific, if ordinary people can master and use this principle, they can save themselves; if sages can master and use it, they can adapt to the changes of world.

This truth can be as vast as the whole universe and as tiny as a cup; you don't need houses to place it or city walls to protect it.

All you have to do is to embrace the truth and remember it by heart to make the enemy state succumb.

According to *Military Prophecy*: "Being both soft and hard helps national prestige to be increasingly strengthened and the state to prosper.

STRATEGY ONE

If you only use softness or weakness, the national strength will be weakened; if you only use hardness or strength, the state will surely perish."
The first and foremost principle of governing a state is to rely on people with both ability and political integrity and to win the support of the people.

To trust sages as our confidants and to use people as our brothers – then you will not make mistakes.

In this way, our actions are like body and joint movements.

More importantly, the use of nature is like the way of heaven; it should be ingenious and effortless.

THREE STRATEGIES OF HUANG SHIGONG

25

The key to unifying the army and governing the state lies in carefully observing the will of the people and correctly implementing these measures: you shall protect those who are in danger, appease those who are afraid, try to call back those who have betrayed, redress those who have been wronged, find those who have complained, promote those who are inferior, suppress those who are arrogant, punish those who are against us, and try to satisfy those who are greedy.

26

Moreover, you shall appoint those who are willing to serve, protect their privacy, be close to those who are good at using strategies, expose those who slander, punish those who slander others, severely punish those who rebel, frustrate those who are insolent, restrain those who are complacent, appease those who are willing to surrender, settle those who are conquered, and forgive those who surrender.

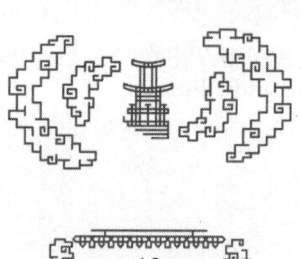

STRATEGY ONE

If you occupy a solid place, you need to guard it;
if you occupy a dangerous place, you need to set up a fortress;
if you occupy a difficult place, you need to garrison it;
if you have a city, you need to give it to the meritorious people;
if you have land, you need to give it to the people who contribute;
if you have property, you need to distribute it to the people.

When the enemy moves, you shall pay attention to their movements;
when the enemy approaches, you shall be on guard;
when the enemy is strong, you shall show weakness to make them arrogant;
when the enemy is at ease, you shall avoid them;
when the enemy comes, you shall fight back resolutely;
when the enemy is fierce, you shall try to avoid them;
when the enemy goes against nature, you shall use justice to denounce them;
when the enemy is harmonious and united, you shall divide them;
you shall comply with the enemy's actions before trying to defeat them.

THREE STRATEGIES OF HUANG SHIGONG

According to the enemy's situation, you shall release false information to make it negligent, and surround it on all sides to annihilate it.

Besides, don't credit yourself only with victories; don't take property as your own; don't take possession of the city for a long time; don't replace the head of state.

Decisions in warfare should be made by you, and credit should be given to the general and soldiers – all of these are benefits for the greater good!
Let others be vassals and you be the king; let them keep their cities and they will levy their own tax.

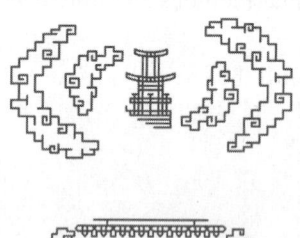

STRATEGY ONE

Kings usually respect their ancestors but rarely take care of their subjects.

Respect for ancestors is only to respect one's relatives, yet only love of the people will make you a wise king.

A monarch who loves his people and values farming does not reduce the farming hours; he reduces taxes and does not make the people poor; he reduces servitude and does not make the people tired.

This way, the state becomes prosperous and the people happy; and then you shall select scholars to manage the people.

THREE STRATEGIES OF HUANG SHIGONG

Wise officials are heroes; therefore, if the enemy's heroes are recruited away, the enemy's state will be in trouble.

Heroes are like the backbone of building a state, and the people are the foundation.

With the backbone standing on a solid foundation, the state will naturally be able to achieve political harmony, peace and prosperity.

The key to the use of troops lies in grand etiquette and a generous salary.

STRATEGY ONE

If you attach great importance to etiquette, men of great ingenuity will automatically come.

With a good salary, the righteous are glad to die with no fear of death.

Therefore, you shall give preferential treatment to the people of virtue, not be stingy with property and reward those who have made contributions in a timely manner.

In this way, your subordinates can work together to weaken the enemy.

THREE STRATEGIES OF HUANG SHIGONG

The way to employ people is to give them proper titles and pay them well; then the wise men will volunteer to serve.

If you receive them with courtesy and encourage them with justice, the righteous man would be willing to die for the state.

A general must share weal and woe with his soldiers.

Only in this way can he attack the enemy and only in this way can the army fully win and the enemy be fully captured.

STRATEGY ONE

Legend has it that there once was a good general who was given a jar of good wine.

He asked his soldiers to pour the wine into the river and drink with them.

Obviously, a jar of wine would not make the river water taste good, but the whole army was convinced to fight for him.

This is because the general could share joys and sorrows with his soldiers.

THREE STRATEGIES OF HUANG SHIGONG

According to *Military Prophecy*: "If the well has not been dug, the general does not say he is thirsty; if the tent has not been set up, the general does not say he is tired; if the stove has not prepared the meals, the general does not say he is hungry.

No fur in winter, no fan in summer as well as no umbrella in rainy days – this is called the general's etiquette.

If a general can share weal and woe with soldiers; his troops are united without separation and can fight continuously without weariness; it is because officers and soldiers love each other and think alike.

That is the way for a general to win the hearts and minds of his soldiers."

STRATEGY ONE

According to *Military Prophecy*: "The reason why the general has the authority lies in his strict and clear command and order.

The reason for complete victory lies in military and political governance.

And the reason why soldiers are not afraid of fighting is because they obey orders." Hence, it is a must that the general send orders and his soldier have faith in reward and punishment.

Orders should be as firm as the existence of heaven and earth.

# THREE STRATEGIES OF HUANG SHIGONG

60

Only when the soldiers obey orders can the army go to war.

61

A general is in charge of commanding the troops and judging combat situations, and soldiers are in charge of fighting against the enemy and achieving victory.

62

Therefore, a general who has no way to govern the army cannot be the commander, and a disloyal army cannot be used to attack the enemy.

63

Because it can neither capture the city nor perish the enemy state; both failures would lead to the weakness of the military.

STRATEGY ONE

The weakness would cause an isolated general and soldiers who do not follow orders.

If such an army is used for defence, it will fail to hold; if it is used to attack, it will be routed – this army is called a declining army, where the general has no prestige and the soldiers are not afraid of punishment.

When the soldiers are not afraid of punishment, the army will be slack; when the army is slack, the soldiers will flee; when soldiers flee, the enemy will take advantage of this opportunity to strike, and the army will be trounced. According to *Military Prophecy*: "A good general shall govern the army and manage the soldiers with a spirit of respect for themselves and others."

THREE STRATEGIES OF HUANG SHIGONG

Rewards help the military grow stronger day by day; their fighting will be as swift as the storm, and their attack as violent as water bursting through riverbank.

Such an army can make the enemy flee and dare not resist; the enemy will surrender rather than fight back.

When a general can lead by example, his army will prevail all over the world.

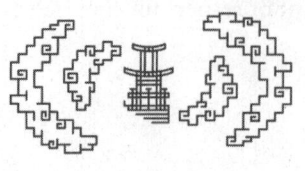

STRATEGY ONE

According to *Military Prophecy*: "Reward and punishment shall not be biased; they shall be handled in a balanced way by alternating the two. When reward and punishment are strictly managed, the general's prestige is established; if the general is competent, the soldiers will be convinced; when the appointees are both virtuous and talented, the enemy state will be crushed."

According to *Military Prophecy*: "The state to which the wise men belong can be invincible." Therefore, a king shall be modest and not arrogant to scholars, not worry the general, and be deliberate in strategy without hesitation.

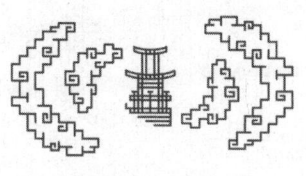

THREE STRATEGIES OF HUANG SHIGONG

If a king is arrogant to scholars, his subordinates will not be obedient;
if a king worries the general, the king and general will not trust each other;
if a king hesitates about strategy, the enemy will take advantage to attack;
if a king goes to war without addressing all the problems, his state will be doomed.

A general is the lifeline of a state.

Only when a general succeeds in leading his troops to defeat the enemy can a state be stable.

STRATEGY ONE

75

According to *Military Prophecy*: "A general shall be be clean, calm, fair, and strict; he shall listen to different opinions; he shall distinguish between right and wrong; he shall recruit talents; he shall learn from all opinions; he shall understand local conditions and the customs of different states; he shall understand the geography of mountains and rivers; he shall know the terrain and obstacles; he shall be able to judge the military conditions."

Therefore, a general shall know the teachings by wise advisers and the foresight of sages, the opinions of the people and of the court, as well as the rise and fall of states.

76

If a general aims at attracting talents, he will follow their advice; however, if he refuses to be persuaded, the talents will leave;

if a general doesn't follow the plan, his advisers will betray him;

if there is no distinction between good and evil, the people who have made contribution tend to be frustrated;

if a general insist on going his own way, his subordinates will blame the superiors;

THREE STRATEGIES OF HUANG SHIGONG

if a general boasts about himself, his subordinates will not contribute;
if a general listens to slander, people will feel alienated;
if a general is greedy, he will not be able to prohibit evil people from causing troubles;
if a general lusts after women, soldiers who are infatuated with women too, will become promiscuous and violate discipline.

If a general has one of the above problems, the military will not trust him.

If he has two, his troops will have no discipline.

If he has three, all the troops will be defeated.

STRATEGY ONE

If he has four, it will bring disaster to the state and the people alike.

According to *Military Prophecy*: "A general's strategy should be kept secret; the soldiers' thinking should be unified, and the attack on enemy should be rapid."
(1) If a general's strategy is secret, spy will not succeed;
(2) if his soldiers' thoughts are unified, the army will be united;
(3) if the attack on enemy is rapid, the enemy will be caught off guard.

With these three "if" rules above, the army's plan will not be disrupted.

THREE STRATEGIES OF HUANG SHIGONG

If a general's strategy is revealed, the army will lose its advantage;
if the enemy can detect your internal condition, calamity is bound to happen;
if illegal goods are smuggled into your barracks, more troubles await.

In summary: If a general has these three problems above, his army is bound to fail.

If a general has no foresight, wise men will leave him;
if a general is not brave, his officers and soldiers will be in fear;
if a general makes a rash move, the morale of the army will be unstable;
when a general vents his anger on others, the whole army will be afraid.

STRATEGY ONE

According to *Military Prophecy*: "Foresight, firmness and bravery are valuable moral characteristics of a general.

The art of leadership for a general is to move the army at the right moment and to express anger at the right moment." Hence, a general shall be cautious about these manners.

According to *Military Prophecy*: "If there is no money in the army, talents will not serve; if there is no reward in the army, the soldiers will not go forward."

According to *Military Prophecy*: "If there is a bait, there must be fish on the hook; if there is great reward, there must be those who dare to die." Therefore, what brings people together is courtesy; and what makes the soldiers happy to die for is reward.

THREE STRATEGIES OF HUANG SHIGONG

Attract them with what they fall for and promise them prizes and rewards, and then soldiers will fight to die.

According to *Military Prophecy*: "A state that wants to deploy an army to fight must first do favours to its soldiers; a state that wants to take an offensive must first let the soldiers rest."

By giving grace, small can trump big, and the weak can beat the strong.

Therefore, a good general should love his soldiers as well as himself in order to make them invincible.

STRATEGY ONE

According to *Military Prophecy*: "The key to use troops is to know the enemy's situation first: the materials in stock, the estimates of food and fodder, the judgement of the strength of the troops, and the observation of weather and terrain, and then to find out the weaknesses of the enemy to take advantage of.

Evidently, if a state transports grain when there is no war, it means that it is short of grain; if the people are pale and skinny, the state is poor.

There is no doubt that people will starve if food is to transported from thousands of *li** away, and that the army won't be able to get enough food to eat without enough firewood to cook.

---

*li is a traditional Chinese unit of distance that is about one third of a mile.

THREE STRATEGIES OF HUANG SHIGONG

If grain is transported from thousands of *li* away, the state will be short of grain for one year.

If grain is transported from two thousand *li* away, it will be short of grain for two years.

If grain is transported from three thousand *li* away, it will be short of grain for three years – this is called a state's weakening strength.

If a state lacks food, its people will be poor; if the people are poor, the upper and lower classes will not stay close together.

STRATEGY ONE

Under such extreme circumstances, the enemy attacks from outside and the people plunder from inside.

As a result, the state will surely collapse and perish."
According to *Military Prophecy*: "When a monarch is tyrannical, his officials will be extremely harsh; when taxes are heavy and penalties are abused, the people will revolt. In this way, the state will perish."

According to *Military Prophecy*: "Underlying corruption, hypocritical integrity, cheating for reputation and embezzling of the imperial government's titles and salaries for personal benefits will makes the upper and the lower classes unaware of the facts; when pretending to be decent and cheating senior officials takes place – this is the beginning of usurpation."

THREE STRATEGIES OF HUANG SHIGONG

104

According to *Military Prophecy*: "Officials form a clique for personal gains and practice cronyism; they send villains to suppress virtuous men; they defy justice in their own interests; colleagues slander and blame each other – this is the root of national trouble."

105

According to *Military Prophecy*: "Rich and powerful clans plot together; although they have no official titles, they enjoy prominent social status to the point that people are scared of them; parties collude with each other to seize the power of the government by buying over people; they oppress the masses and cause uproars, but the officials deceive the king and dare not speak out – this is the root cause of disasters."

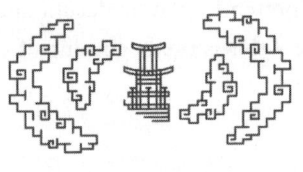

STRATEGY ONE

106

According to *Military Prophecy*: "They do evil from generation to generation and erode the authority of the king; everything they do is for their own convenience; they even try to distort the laws, threatening the authority of the monarch – these people are considered as traitors."

107

According to *Military Prophecy*: "When there are more officials than the people; when there is no distinction between upper and lower classes; when bullying is endemic and there is no way to stop – all these will inevitably affect the virtuous men, and the state will suffer as well."

108

According to *Military Prophecy*: "If good people are respected without being appointed in office; if villains are detested without being sacked; if the talented and virtuous retire and the indecent are in power – then the state will suffer."

THREE STRATEGIES OF HUANG SHIGONG

109

According to *Military Prophecy*: "The imperial family is powerful and form a clique to occupy important positions; they dare to offend the both the upper and the lower classes while the king does not try to get rid of them – then the state will suffer."

110

According to *Military Prophecy*: "The whole army will be indignant when the sycophants are in power.

111

These people throw their weight around to show off and to act against the will of the public.

112

These people don't have integrity and principles, for they only seek to please the superiors; they are self-important and boastful.

STRATEGY ONE

113

They arbitrarily slander men of great morality and frame up men of accomplishments.

114

They do not deal with government affairs timely to the point that the orders from above do not get passed down.

115

They practice harsh policies and tamper with traditions and the common law.

116

A monarch is bound to suffer if he employs such people as officials."

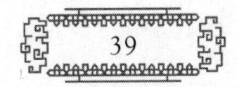

THREE STRATEGIES OF HUANG SHIGONG

117

According to *Military Prophecy*: "Wicked men praise each other to try to fool the king, so that the king cannot tell right from wrong.

118

They slander and flatter at the same time to try to fool the king, so that the king cannot tell virtue from evil.

119

They practice cronyism, so that the king loses his loyal officers."
Therefore, the king must be able to see through the appearances and find out the seeds of trouble;
if the king uses virtuous talents, then sycophants will be driven away;
if the king uses virtuous talents, everything will be in order;
if the king employs hermits, the talents will be enriched;
if the king draws upon the wisdom of the common people, he will win the hearts of the people and leave remarkable political legacy;
with the support of the public, the king's benevolence can be felt from afar.

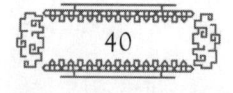

CHAPTER II.

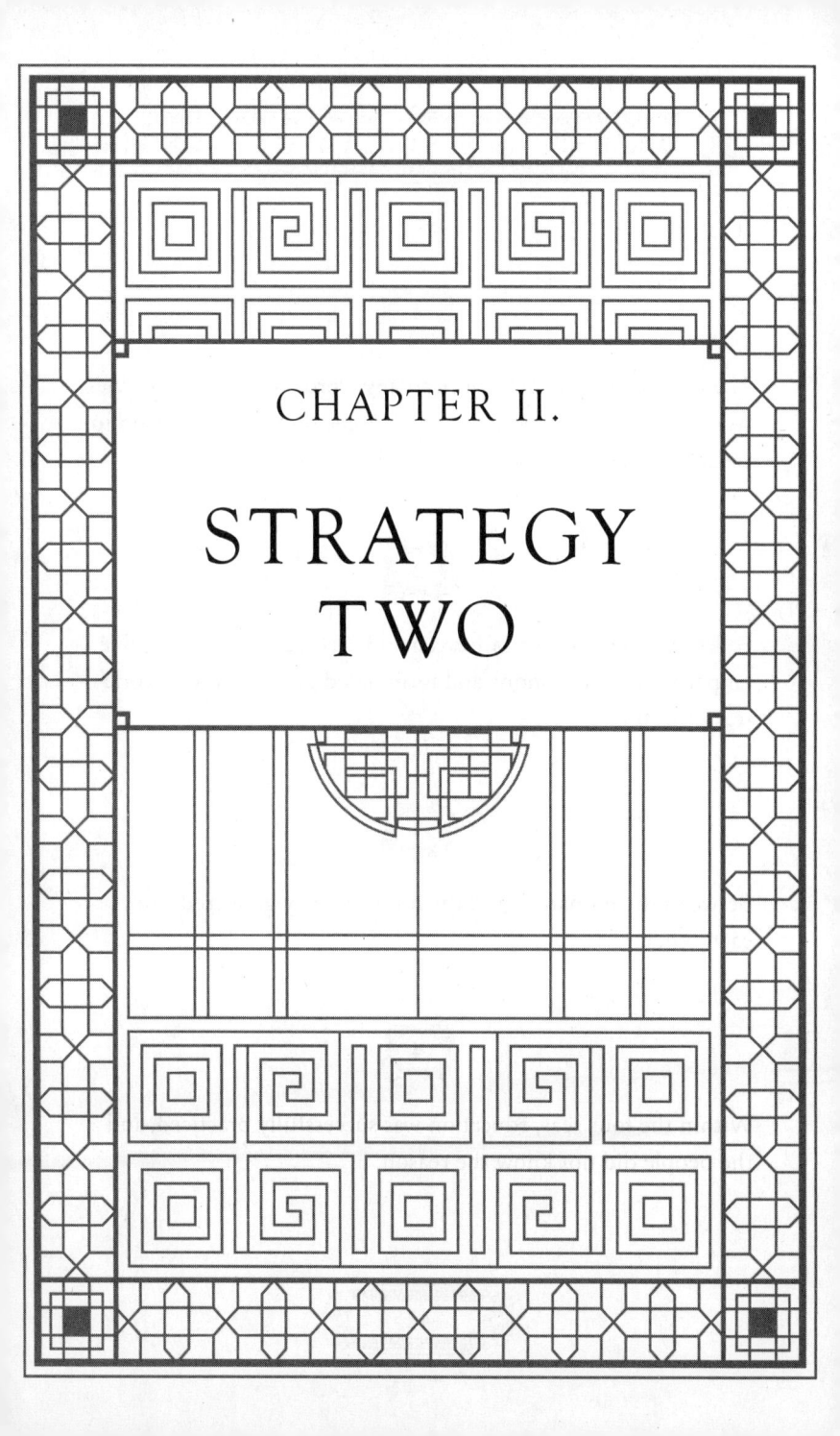

STRATEGY TWO

THREE STRATEGIES OF HUANG SHIGONG

1

The three emperors did not need any words, and their doctrines were learned everywhere; and the people didn't know whom to credit with the successes achieved.

2

Following the example of heaven and earth, the succeeding five emperors added sermons and formulated decrees, so the world was peaceful.

3

Between the monarchs and the minister, they gave credit to each other.

4

Within the four seas, education was successfully practiced, and the people did not know the reason.

STRATEGY TWO

5

Therefore, the use of officials did not rely on courtesy and reward to achieve harmony between them and the monarchs.

6

The three emperors governed and convinced the people with morality; they drafted laws and regulations to prevent the system from disintegration.

7

Their vassals made pilgrimages on time, and the laws were well-implemented.

8

Despite the build-up of armaments, there was no threat of war.

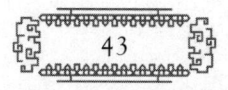

THREE STRATEGIES OF HUANG SHIGONG

9

The monarchs did not doubt their ministers, and the ministers did not doubt the monarchs either.

10

Their states were stable and their authority was consolidated.

11

When a minister retired, he could live in harmony without any suspicion with the kings.

12

Later on, the five hegemons ruled by making friends with, trusting, employing and rewarding them; but without trust, officials would be alienated and without reward, they would not be dedicated.

STRATEGY TWO

13

According to *Military Prophecy*: "The most important thing in sending troops into battle is that the general shall be the single commander."

14

If the advance and the retreat of the army are under the full control of a monarch instead, it is difficult to win.

15

According to *Military Prophecy*: "The wise, the brave, the greedy and the stupid are employed in different ways.

16

Wise people prefer to make contributions; brave people prefer to realise their ambitions; greedy people prefer to pursue wealth, and stupid people do not hesitate to die.

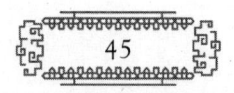

THREE STRATEGIES OF HUANG SHIGONG

17

To use them according to their own characteristics is the subtle trick of employing people."

18

According to *Military Prophecy*: "Do not let the eloquent talk about the strengths of the enemy, because that will cause confusion.

19

Do not use a kind person to manage finance, because he will waste money by bending to the demands of his subordinates."

20

According to *Military Prophecy*: "Witchcraft should be forbidden completely in the army, and it is not allowed to practice divination for the soldiers."

STRATEGY TWO

21

According to *Military Prophecy*: "The use of chivalrous people has nothing to do with money.

22

The righteous will not work for the unrighteous, and the wise will not assist an incompetent king."

23

The monarch cannot be an immoral man, for his ministers will betray him; he cannot be a man without authority and influence, for he will lose his power as a result.

24

A minister cannot be an immoral man, for he will be unable to assist the king; a minister cannot be a man without authority and influence, for the state will be on decline as a result.

THREE STRATEGIES OF HUANG SHIGONG

25

However, if a minister's power is excessive, it does not bode well for his future.

26

Therefore, a wise king governs the world, observes the ups and downs of times, weights the gains and losses of personnel, and then formulates the rules and regulations.

27

Feudal lords are in charge of two armies, local earls have three, and the Son of Heaven has six.

28

When the state is in in turmoil, rebellion comes into being.

STRATEGY TWO

29

When the virtue of the king disappears, an alliance of lords and mutual attacks take place.

30

The lords are comparable to each other by strength and no one is strong enough to defeat another, so they strive to recruit warriors and practice strategies.

31

Therefore, there is no way to resolve suspicion without planning; there is no way to conquer traitors without deceit; and there is no way to succeed without secret planning.

32

Sages can understand the way of heaven; virtuous men can follow the geography of terrain; and wise men can learn from the past.

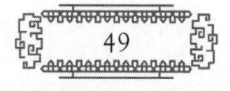

THREE STRATEGIES OF HUANG SHIGONG

33

Therefore, *Three Strategies* is a book written for a time of depression.

34

Strategy One is to set up a system of reward and punishment, to identify the good and the evil, and to reveal the reasons of success or failure.

35

Strategy Two is to distinguish between virtues and misconducts and to perceive the art of leadership.

36

Strategy Three is to describe morality, to examine safety and danger, and to explain the sin of doing harm to virtuous people.

STRATEGY TWO

37

Therefore, when a king is good with Strategy One, he can appoint the wise to subdue the enemy.

38

With a deep understanding of Strategy Two, a king can manage generals and command troops.

39

With a thorough knowledge of Strategy Three, a king can clearly identify the root causes of prosperity and decline, and be familiar with the disciplines of state governance.

40

When ministers are well versed in the art of Strategy Two, they can accomplish great achievements and preserve their wealth.

THREE STRATEGIES OF HUANG SHIGONG

41

When the high-flying bird is dead, the good bow should be put away.

42

When an enemy state is destroyed, the advisors are not needed anymore.

43

To eliminate advisors is not to destroy their bodies, but to weaken their prestige and to deprive them of power.

44

On the imperial court, they shall be awarded the highest title among other ministers to acknowledge their contributions; they shall be granted fertile lands in the Central Plain to make their family rich, and they shall be given beauties and treasures to make them happy.

STRATEGY TWO

45

Once the army is formed, it cannot be disbanded in a hurry.

46

Once military power is granted, it cannot be withdrawn immediately.

47

At the end of the war, the general returns from the front.

48

And this moment is a matter of life and death for the monarch's future.

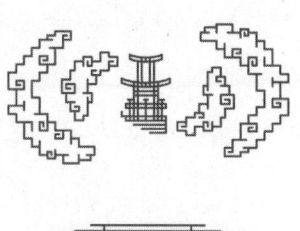

THREE STRATEGIES OF HUANG SHIGONG

49

He shall weaken the general's strength in the name of feudal nobility, and deprive his military power in the name of feudal territory.

50

This is the scheme adopted by rulers to govern their generals for ages.

51

Hence, decisions made by rulers are diverse and multi-faceted.

52

Preserving state and recruiting heroes is the art of leadership discussed in Strategy Two.

STRATEGY TWO

53

The monarchs of all dynasties have been taking this principle as a secret way of governance.

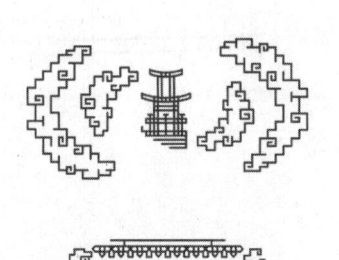

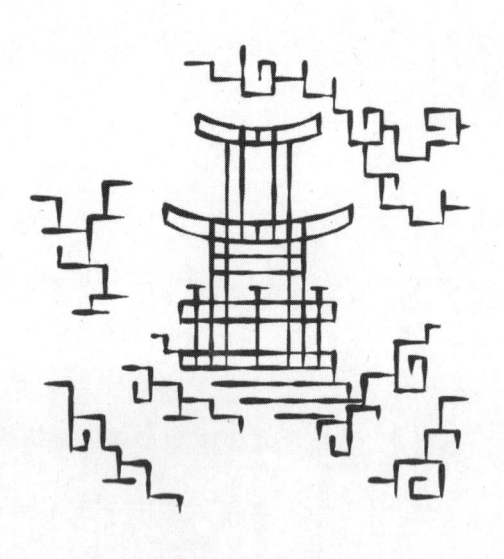

CHAPTER III.

STRATEGY THREE

THREE STRATEGIES OF HUANG SHIGONG

1

Those who can save the world from danger will get peace.

2

Those who can relieve worries from the world can enjoy happiness.

3

Those who can save the state from disaster can embrace blessings.

4

Therefore, if a king's grace is all over his people, sages will follow him; if his grace is all over things under heaven, sages will turn to him.

STRATEGY THREE

5

The state will be strong if the wise gather to serve; the world can be unified if sages gather to serve.

6

It is necessary to use the "Virtue" to team up with the wise and the "Way" to team up with sages.

7

If the wise leave, the state will be weak; if sages leave, the state will be in chaos.

8

Weakness leads to danger, and chaos is the sign of impending collapse of the state.

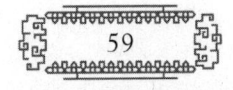

THREE STRATEGIES OF HUANG SHIGONG

9

When a wise man is in power, he can make people obey by action; when a sage is in power, he can make people obey from the bottom of their heart.

10

If the people obey by action, the king can carry out reforms; if the people obey from the bottom of their heart, the king can govern well from the start to the end.

11

It is etiquette education that requires people to obey by action, and it is music education that motivates people to obey.

12

Music education here does not really refer to the use of musical instruments, but to the education that nurtures love for families, clans, occupations, cities, national decrees, and social ethics.

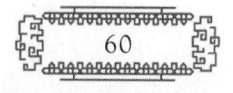

STRATEGY THREE

13

In this way, a king can govern his people, and then make music to nurture his people, so that the society will enjoy lasting harmony.

14

Therefore, a monarch with morality uses music to make the world happy; a monarch without morality uses music to make only himself happy.

15

Those who make the world happy will have long-term stability; those who make only themselves happy will soon perish.

16

Those who do not practice internal affairs but expand outwards will try in vain.

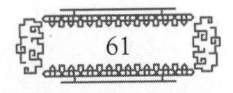

THREE STRATEGIES OF HUANG SHIGONG

17

By contrast, those who do not expand but cultivate internal affairs will achieve success at ease.

18

Those who implement policies to promote people's well-being, will be loved by the people and the state will have loyal ministers.

19

Those who implement policies that wear down people and waste money will be criticised by the people and there will be plenty resentful subjects.

20

Therefore, those who are keen to expand territory will inevitably abandon their internal affairs; conversely, those who do their best to cultivate their virtue will be strong.

STRATEGY THREE

21

A state will be safe if efforts are paid to safeguard what it already has; a state will be in ruins if each one covets what others have and their future generations will suffer from a cruel and brutal tyranny.

22

As things go beyond the limit, even if they succeed for a while, they will inevitably fail.

23

If people do not correct themselves but correct others instead, they act against the norm, because it only makes sense to correct themselves first and then correct others.

24

Disobedience is the root of trouble and disorder; after all, obedience to common sense is the key to national stability.

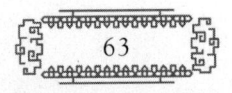

THREE STRATEGIES OF HUANG SHIGONG

25

The Way, morality, benevolence, righteousness and etiquette are integrated to be one.

26

The Way is what people should follow;
morality is what people get from the Way;
benevolence is what people feel close to;
righteousness is what people should do;
and etiquette is the code of conduct.
Not a single one of these five can be omitted.

27

Therefore, to live with manners is the restraint of etiquette;
to get revenge is a decision of righteousness;
compassion is the beginning of benevolence;
cultivating oneself as well as others is the road to morality;
putting everyone on an equal footing and assigning them proper positions is the enlightenment of the Way.

STRATEGY THREE

28

A monarch issues "instruction" to his subordinates.

29

When the instruction is written on bamboo, it is called "order."

30

The execution of order is called "duty."

31

A wrong instruction will affect implementation of order, which will further deviate duty; and the Way of state governance cannot be well-established.

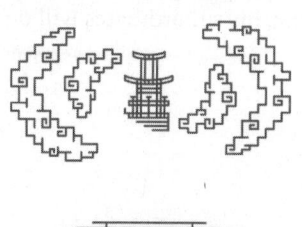

THREE STRATEGIES OF HUANG SHIGONG

32

Consequently, evil officials will rise to power and the prestige of the monarch will be damaged.

33

It takes as far as thousands of *li* to find and hire wise men, while it takes short way to attract the unworthy people.

34

Therefore, a wise monarch always goes thousands of *li* to seek wise officials and ignore the villains closer to him.

35

Therefore, if a king can preserve his achievements by appointing the wise and capable, his subordinates will do their best.

STRATEGY THREE

36

If a wise man is abandoned, many more wise officials will retire.

37

If one villain is rewarded, many more villains will come.

38

If virtuous men are protected and wicked men are punished, the state will be stable and all the virtuous men will come to serve.

39

If the people have doubts about the decree, the state will not be stable; if the people are confused by the decree, the society will not be governed.

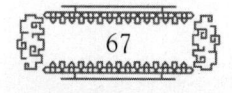

THREE STRATEGIES OF HUANG SHIGONG

40

When doubts disappear and confusion is relieved, the state will be peaceful.

41

If one decree goes against public opinion, other decrees cannot be implemented; if one terrible policy is implemented, terrible consequences will follow.

42

Therefore, a king shall run a benevolent government for the obedient people and severely punish the unruly people.

43

In this way, the government order will be duly obeyed and no one will complain.

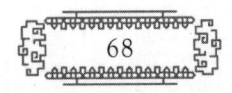

STRATEGY THREE

44

It is a violation of the way of heaven to govern the resentful people with the decrees that people denounce.

45

If the government decrees detested by the people are used to govern those people, disasters will be imminent.

46

The governance of the people depends on the balance between the rich and the poor, and the balance between the rich and the poor depends on political clarity.

47

In this way, the people will have their own place and the world will be peaceful.

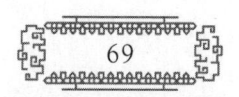

THREE STRATEGIES OF HUANG SHIGONG

48

If those who commit crimes are the noble class and those who receive bribery become richer, then even a wise king is unable to govern the state well.

49

Those who commit crimes shall be punished and those who receive bribery shall by put behind bars.

50

Only in this way can etiquette be adhered to and all kinds of evils naturally disappear.

51

A man of great morality cannot be bought over with title and money; a man of great discipline cannot be threatened with power and punishment.

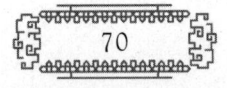

STRATEGY THREE

52

Therefore, a wise monarch seeks virtuous men by considering their will and interests.

53

To hire people with great morality, a king should pay attention to etiquette; to hire people with integrity, a king should advocate principles.

54

In this way, the wise can be hired, and the king's reputation can be preserved.

55

Virtuous men can understand the root causes of the rise and fall of things; they know the signs of success and failure, the key to the control of chaos and when to stay and when to resign.

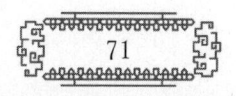

THREE STRATEGIES OF HUANG SHIGONG

56

Even when they suffer poverty, they do not covet the high positions of a declining state or try to profit from a troubled state.

57

Those who live as hermits but excel in state governance shall be assigned important positions once the time comes.

58

When the monarch's ambition is constant with their own, they can contribute to outstanding achievements.

59

And their art of governance will be cherished for the many generations to come.

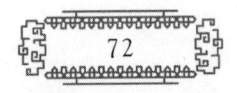

STRATEGY THREE

60

When a monarch goes to war, it is not out of his own interest, but to quell cruelty and rebellion.

61

To fight against injustice with justice is like drowning a small torch with a river, or pushing down a tottering man beside a bottomless abyss.

62

The victory is inevitable.

63

The reason why a wise monarch is quiet and calm and does not rush to battle is that he does not want to cause too much loss of personnel and materials.

THREE STRATEGIES OF HUANG SHIGONG

64

War is ominous; and the way of heaven is against war.

65

Only wage a war when it is necessary; that is in accordance with the way of heaven.

66

The relationship between man and heaven is like that between fish and water.

67

Fish survive in water and die without.

68

Therefore, wise men are always in awe and dare not deviate from the way of heaven for a moment.

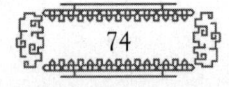

STRATEGY THREE

69

When autocratic ministers are in power, the prestige of the monarch will be hurt.

70

The decision of life and death is made by those ministers; as a result, the power of the monarch is exhausted.

71

Only when the autocratic officials bow to orders can the state last long.

72

Only when the decision of life and death is controlled by the king can the state be stable.

THREE STRATEGIES OF HUANG SHIGONG

73

If the people are poor, the state has no reserves.

74

If the people are rich, the state will be secure.

75

When the wise and talented are appointed, wicked men will be excluded.

76

When the wicked are appointed, the wise will die.

77

Without a strict sense of hierarchy, disasters will further affect the later generations.

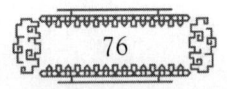

STRATEGY THREE

78

When a minister compares himself to a ruler, all the treacherous people will take advantage of the opportunity to gather.

79

When a minister enjoys the dignity of a ruler, the name of the ruler and his subjects becomes obscure and unclear.

80

When a ruler is reduced to the status of a vassal, the order of things above and below him will be reversed and confused.

81

He who harms a wise man will have his misfortune spread to three generations of his children.

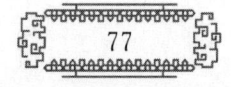

THREE STRATEGIES OF HUANG SHIGONG

82

He who ignores a virtuous man will have his own retribution.

83

He who envies a virtuous man will not have his honour preserved.

84

He who recommends a virtuous man will benefit from his good deeds for generations to come.

85

So, a wise man is always eager to recommend the virtuous, and thus his reputation is made famous.

STRATEGY THREE

86

If only one person benefits and one hundred suffer, the people will leave the city or town.

87

If it is good for one person and harmful for ten thousand, the state will be divided.

88

Remove one man and benefit a hundred, and the people will admire the king's kindness.

89

Get rid of one man in favour of ten thousand, and there will be no disorder in politics.

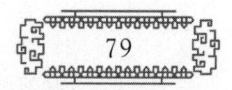

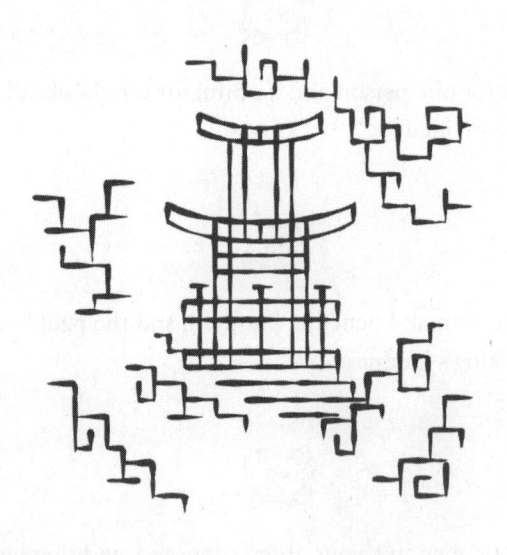